D8676814

WORLD MYTHS AND LEGENDS II

Europe

Ellen Dolan
Frederick McKissack, Jr.

Globe
Fearon

Upper Saddle River,
New Jersey

World Myths and Legends
Greek and Roman
Ancient Middle Eastern
Norse
African
Far Eastern
Celtic
Native American
Regional American

World Myths and Legends II
India
Russia
Europe
South America
The Caribbean
Central America
Mexico
Southeast Asia

Series Editor: Joseph T. Curran
Cover Designer: Dianne Platner
Text Designer: Teresa A. Holden
Interior Illustrations: Carol Stutz
Cover Photo: The Granger Collection, New York

Library of Congress Catalog Card Number: 92–72305

ISBN 0–822–44646–4

Printed in the United States of America
3 4 5 6 7 8 9 10 04 03 02 01 00

EB

CONTENTS

*An Introduction to the Myths
and Legends of Europe*   v

1   Tales of Heroes

How Finland Began *(Finland)*   1
El Cid's Last Battle *(Spain)*   8
William Tell *(Switzerland)*   15
The Boy Who Held Back the Sea
   (The Netherlands)   26

2   Animal Tales

Reynard the Fox *(France)*   34
The Lark and the Wolf *(Poland)*   39
Dinner in the Woods *(Ukraine)*   49

3   Tales of Magic

The Beautiful Rose *(France)*   57
The Song of the Lorelei *(Germany)*   67
The Secret of Mélusine *(France)*   73

4   Folktales

Till Feeds the Town *(Germany)*   82

Clever Manka *(Czechoslovakia)*   92

The Wooden Bowl *(Italy)*   98

The Clockmaker of Strassburg
    (Germany)   104

Pronunciation Guide   113

An Introduction to the Myths and Legends of Europe

Long before there were films, televisions, radios, or books, people told stories. Many of the ones in this book are hundreds of years old. Most of the myths and legends in this book were first told in Europe in the Middle Ages. This was a period of time from the twelfth century through the sixteenth century.

Families told the stories by firesides as evening entertainment. Sometimes the stories were told as moral lessons that everyone could understand. Many stories were passed along in inns and taverns. The stories went from town to town as merchants, visitors, and families took them on their travels.

Since the stories were told many times before they were written down, they occasionally changed. A different storyteller would add some details he or she liked. Sometimes storytellers changed a part to reflect current attitudes and beliefs. Consequently, many of the stories in this book have versions in several countries. The stories differ somewhat from country to country, but the main ideas remain constant. Stories about Reynard the Fox, for example, probably originated in Germany. There are stories about Reynard in French folklore as well. Reynard, however, is the same type of trickster in all the stories. Stories about the pranks of Till Eulenspiegel range from Germany, where they probably began, to Belgium and England.

Myths and legends reflect the events of the times in which they were first told. The Middle Ages was a time when there were many conflicts in Europe. At that time, the present boundaries of the European countries had not been established. Groups who wanted to own and govern large areas of land fought one another bitterly. There are stories in this book that take place during some of those wars. Examples of battling heroes are El Cid, the Spanish soldier, and William Tell, the symbol of Swiss nationalism. Their stories are in the first section, about heroes.

Every country has stories of how the world began. The creation story in this book is from Finland. It is in the section about heroes because its main character is a hero.

He is the mythical character who planned Finland's many beautiful forests and lakes.

The second section of the book contains stories about animals. Animals that act like humans are common in the myths and legends of all cultures. These stories have lessons for humans. The stories are about not being greedy, the value of cooperation, and not believing rumors too quickly.

Magic is a common element in the folktales of Europe. The third section of the book contains stories about magical events. There are creatures who change from beasts to attractive humans. There is a magically appearing horse-drawn chariot. There is a romantic creature who can build a castle with small amounts of water and stone.

The last section of the book includes folktales about people who, though fictional, are quite believable. The characters are ordinary people who solve problems or show special consideration for others.

The stories in this book represent many different cultures in Europe. There are stories of fantasy, of romance, of heroism, and of struggle. Although the stories were first told hundreds of years ago, most are still popular today.

How Finland Began

A long poem, The Kalevala, meaning "Land of the Heroes," tells ancient stories about Finland. The work was published in 1835 by a doctor who had traveled to many towns gathering the stories. This is the first story. It tells of the creation of life on Earth and of the land of Finland.

Water Mother

In the beginning, the world was filled only with swirling air. It was cold, dark, and very quiet. After a time, a woman came out from the swirls of air. Her hair was long and silvery. Her garments were thin and light as the mist. For a time the woman drifted through the air and thought of all the things she had to do.

First the woman created a child who was called Water. Water became all the seas and lakes and rivers. Then the woman thought of more. She fluttered her right hand and created White Bird. She fluttered her left hand and created Black Bird. From then on, there would be creatures in this quiet world.

When the woman grew tired of drifting in the air, she sank into the water and rested. From that time on, she was known as Water Mother.

White Bird circled above Water Mother and called, "There is water everywhere. I cannot find a place to lay my eggs. What shall I do?"

"I will bend my knees above the water," replied Water Mother. "You may put your eggs on my knees."

So White Bird laid her eggs and sat on them to keep them warm. At first the eggs were just warm, but then they became hot. When Water Mother could no longer stand the heat, she pulled her knees back under the cool water. The cold water on the hot eggs caused the eggs to crack, and they fell apart.

"What have you done to my fine eggs?" asked White Bird.

"I did not mean to break them," Water Mother said. "Perhaps I can find a use for the cracked eggs."

Quickly Water Mother swept up the shells and the insides of the eggs. Then she began to work. From the bottoms of the eggs, Water Mother made the earth. From the tops of the eggs, she made the sky. She turned the egg yellows into the sun and the egg whites into the moon. The tiny speckled parts became the stars. Black bits from the eggs became the clouds.

"So we have the rounded earth and the circle of sky," Water Mother said. "We have night and day. There are many places now for you to lay eggs, White Bird."

Water Mother's Son

Water Mother continued her work. On the earth, she shaped hills and mountains. She smoothed flat plains so that rivers could carry water from the mountains to the sea. She created animals and plants and then people for the earth. Only then did she herself give birth to a human child. This was her son, Väinämöinen. He was born in the cool, calm water. Väinämöinen was Water Mother's last gift to the world.

Väinämöinen had waited a long time to be born. He had waited so long that by the time it happened he was an old man. He had a long white beard. These things did not matter, though. Väinämöinen had been given the most favored gift of all—song.

After his birth, Väinämöinen bounced

The land Water Mother made

about in the water for a time. Then he began to swim toward land. He pulled himself ashore, squeezed water from his beard, and looked about the new world.

"Where are the trees?" he asked. "I must have tall, fine trees."

A small man who was born of the earth came toward him.

"I have many seeds," the man said. "I can plant any number you want."

Väinämöinen was already thinking in large amounts.

"Plant hundreds and hundreds," he said in his loud, singing voice.

In a short time, there were many trees. There were enough trees to please even Väinämöinen. One oak tree grew faster and larger than any of the others. It shut out the sky and the sun. That made the world dark again.

Väinämöinen walked along the shore. He sang out across the water, "Our world is dark and sad. Please send someone big enough to cut down the oak tree."

Väinämöinen waited, but no one answered. Just as he turned to leave, the waters began to move. Around and around they whirled. Väinämöinen thought there was a monster in the whirlpool, or perhaps it was a big fish. It was neither. A tiny man dressed in copper armor rose from the water. Väinämöinen picked him up with one hand and laughed until his beard shook.

"Ha!" said Väinämöinen. "Here is another small man. Are you the answer to my call? How can you cut down a tree?"

The little man waved his little ax. It was no bigger than a penny.

"I may be small," he said. "Yet I will cut down the tree."

All at once the man began to grow. He grew taller and wider. The ax grew with him. When his head reached the clouds, the man swung the ax. He swung again and once again. The tree fell over with a crash, and there was light again in the land. Before Väinämöinen could say anything, the man went back to the sea. The water swirled, and the man quickly disappeared. Once again, a small man had been a great help in making the earth Väinämöinen wanted.

Väinämöinen cleared part of the forest and planted seeds. They began to grow, and before long, there were fields of waving grain. Väinämöinen had planned and built the beautiful land of Finland.

Since much of the work was now done, Väinämöinen rested. He sat with his back to a tree. He lifted his head and began to sing.

Väinämöinen sang of air and water. He sang of earth and sun, of trees and grain. He sang of ancient wisdom. He sang of things yet to be. The songs floated far out over the mountains and far out over the seas. From Väinämöinen's beautiful singing, all the world heard about the wonders of Finland.

1. *What did Water Mother make with the egg yellows?*
2. *What was Väinämöinen's special gift?*
3. *Why did Väinämöinen want the oak tree cut down?*

El Cid's Last Battle

There are many stories from Spain about El Cid. They are based on a real person who lived in the eleventh century. This was a time when there were many battles for land in Spain. These were battles between groups of Spanish soldiers and also between the Spanish and the Moors. The Moors had originally come from Africa and Asia and had conquered many places in Spain.

This story takes place after a battle with the Moors. In it El Cid has been seriously wounded in the battle.

The people of Valencia gathered at the city gates. "Welcome home!" they cried. "Welcome, El Cid! Thank you for saving Valencia."

The cheers were for the soldiers who had just won a battle with the Moors. The Spanish leader, El Cid, was a brave and popular soldier who had won many battles before.

With El Cid's leadership, the army had managed to keep control of their city. Many soldiers had suffered injuries, however, and El Cid himself was hurt.

El Cid's wife Jimena was among those who greeted the soldiers at the city gates. As she helped her husband get down from his horse, she realized that he was badly wounded. She called for help in taking the hero to his bed in the palace.

"Don't worry," El Cid said slowly. "It's only my shoulder. I will be able to defend Valencia when the Moors return."

"You must rest," Jimena said. "Your shoulder is broken, and you have bruises all over. You have saved the city. Now others can defend it."

El Cid was pale, and every word he spoke seemed to cause him great pain. When they got to the palace, he lay down on his bed and tried to sleep. Jimena sat by his side.

During the night, El Cid was restless and feverish. He called out as if he were in battle. He tried to sit up, but each time he fell back with an agonizing cry.

By morning, Jimena had called a doctor. The doctor shook his head sadly. He said that El Cid would probably never fight again.

Suddenly El Cid cried out, "Valencia! Spain forever!" Then he was quiet. Jimena held his hand, and the doctor leaned over him. El Cid had died.

Word spread through the palace and then throughout the city. The people began to fear for their safety since their greatest soldier was gone. Cries rang out all over Valencia.

"El Cid is dead! El Cid is dead!"

"What will we do? How will we escape an attack by the Moors?"

"We will all be killed!"

"Who will lead us now?"

The news of El Cid's death also spread outside the city. The Moors were happy to hear the news, and they immediately began planning to attack Valencia. They began to gather outside the city gates. They marched around in a threatening way. The people inside became very frightened.

Even as she grieved, Jimena thought of a plan. Perhaps El Cid could once again save the people of Valencia.

"We can protect ourselves and honor El Cid," she declared.

While El Cid's body was being prepared for burial, Jimena explained her plan. Then the soldiers began to help her carry it out. They brought in all of El Cid's armor. They carefully dressed him as if he were going back into battle. Then they helped Jimena lift El Cid's body and take him out into the courtyard.

"Bring us El Cid's horse!" one person ordered.

"Bring strong ropes!" shouted another.

Jimena carefully pushed open the dead man's eyelids. El Cid now stared ahead as if still determined to fight. His armor made him again look like a soldier. His faithful horse stood ready for her rider.

Then Jimena and the soldiers lifted El Cid onto his horse. They tied his body into the saddle. They tied his feet to the stirrups. They placed his sword in his hand. El Cid was ready to lead the Spanish soldiers yet one more time.

The soldiers mounted their own horses and prepared to ride behind El Cid.

"Open the gates!" they called. "We will meet the forces of the Moors proudly. We will follow El Cid."

The gates were opened. Someone gave El Cid's horse a slap and away they all rode through the city gates.

The soldiers outside the city could not believe what they saw. An army they had thought was too sick to fight came forth from

El Cid prepares for his last battle

the city. Leading them was a man they had thought was dead, sitting straight and tall on his horse.

"That looks like El Cid!" the Moors cried. "El Cid is dead. How can this be?"

One of the soldiers lifted his sword and threw it at El Cid. It struck El Cid in the chest. El Cid rode on. Another soldier raised his sword, but then he looked closely at the tall figure. El Cid's eyes stared without moving while a sword was stuck in his body. He was a fearful sight.

"That is El Cid's ghost!" a soldier shouted.

"We will never escape from El Cid!" said others.

The Moors were so shocked by the sight that they lay down their swords and ran. Many of them feared that they would never be able to defeat the Spanish. They worried that even in death El Cid would be present at every battle.

The Spanish soldiers marched through the army of the Moors with hardly a scratch. The Moors fled from Valencia.

Jimena's plan had saved the city.

1. *How had El Cid been injured?*
2. *What was Jimena's plan?*
3. *What did the Moors do when they heard of El Cid's death?*

William Tell

William Tell is a legendary hero of Switzerland. In the 1300s, this land was ruled by the strong Austrian Hapsburg kings. The kings did not try to understand the lives of poor people in small villages. They merely wanted to collect gold, jewels, grain, and money as taxes from the people. After years of fear and suffering, the villagers grew tired of the Austrian bullies. They decided to fight back. William Tell's adventures became the symbol for Swiss freedom.

Long ago William Tell lived with his family in a land that is now Switzerland. This was a place of enormous mountains and beautiful clear lakes.

William was so strong that he moved rocks around the pasture as if they were pebbles. He dug the fields as quickly as a dog burying a bone. He could easily bend a crossbow and send an arrow straight to its target.

William had courage as well as a strong arm and a sharp eye. He spoke out against the heavy taxes people had to pay with their money and food.

"These taxes are not fair," William said. "Our people work hard to grow food and raise animals. The tax collector takes far too much for himself."

William's speeches made him many friends in the village. The speeches also made a powerful enemy, however, the tax collector named Gessler. Gessler took enough money from the people to build a large house for himself.

Gessler had a band of soldiers to help him collect food and money. They collected the taxes on horseback and rowed boats across the lake to Gessler's fine house.

When Gessler did not receive as much as he wished, he became angry. He would go to the villagers and demand more.

"Look at this small amount of bread, only ten loaves," Gessler said to the baker. "My men and I will have this eaten by morning. You must give us more."

"I need at least twenty loaves for the villagers' breakfasts," said the baker.

"Nonsense," said the tax collector. "Five will be plenty for the villagers. We will take the rest."

Gessler repeated his unreasonable demands all through the village. It was the same with fish and meat and eggs. It did not matter if it was the last bit of food in a villager's home. No matter how much Gessler took, it never seemed to be enough for him.

The villagers grew tired of this tyranny, but they did not know how to stop it. They began to meet in secret and to discuss how they might deal with Gessler. William Tell often joined these meetings.

Somehow Gessler heard of the secret meetings. He made a plan to discover which people were against him. He told his soldiers to put up a tall pole in the middle of the village square. Then he took off his hat with the large brim.

"Hang this hat on top of the pole," Gessler said. "Each person who passes must bow in front of my hat. If anyone will not, throw that person in jail."

Gessler was pleased with his clever plan to find the troublemakers. Many of the villagers were afraid of the soldiers and did not want to go to jail. So each time they passed the pole, they bowed low.

One morning William Tell and his son Jem came down to the village to buy supplies. Jem went to get some fruit, and

William crossed the square to the market. The soldiers stepped out in front of him.

"You must bow low before the tax collector's hat," the soldiers said.

"What?" William asked. "You must be mad. I would not bow to the tax collector himself. I certainly will not bow to his hat."

William marched on across the square.

"Stop!" shouted a soldier. "You are under arrest."

It took three more soldiers to help tie William's hands behind his back. Then they struggled off to jail with him. Jem was left behind and wandered sadly back to the square.

A messenger went to tell Gessler. The tax collector smiled when he heard William Tell was in jail. He hurried to town because he had a plan to make William suffer even more. He called for William to be brought to the center of the town square. He had the soldiers find Jem and bring him also.

"It is said that you are very good with your bow and arrow," Gessler said to William. "I hear you can shoot a flying crow or a running weasel without fail. Now, I wish to see your great skill."

Gessler reached out and took an apple

from the basket of a villager. He held it up for all to see. Then he called Jem to stand beside his father.

"I will place this apple on the head of your fine son," Gessler said. "You will choose one arrow from the quiver you carry. Then you will shoot the apple off your son's head. If you do not, I will have both of you killed!"

William was angry at the tax collector. He was afraid for his son. He started to object by leaving quickly, but the soldiers closed in and blocked any escape. William saw that he must obey.

The soldiers pulled out ropes to tie Jem to a tree. William's hands began to shake. How could he shoot at his own son? He realized, however, that if he did not, the soldiers would kill both of them.

When the soldiers prepared to tie Jem, Jem stepped away from them.

"As the son of William Tell," Jem stated, "I was born free. Even if I am to die, I wish to remain free. You do not need to tie me."

Jem stepped to the tree and faced across the square. William was encouraged by his son's bravery. He emptied his quiver of arrows on the ground. Carefully William chose the straightest one. Then he slid a second arrow under his shirt, where Gessler could not see it.

Gessler handed the apple to a soldier who placed it on Jem's head. Jem stood straight and still. The villagers waited quietly. Some could not bear to watch and turned their heads away.

William carefully fitted an arrow into its slot on his bow. Then with strong, steady arms, he raised the bow, aimed, and pulled. Swish! The arrow flew across the square. It hit the apple exactly and went through it to stick in the tree. The apple fell to the ground in two pieces. Jem was safe.

The villagers cheered, but Gessler was more angry than ever. He tried to think of how he could have William Tell locked up for good. As Gessler thought of that, he saw William bend to put his arm around his son. William's shirt fell open, showing the hidden arrow.

"What are you doing with that extra arrow?" Gessler demanded. "You were only allowed one."

William straightened and looked directly into Gessler's eyes. He spoke slowly.

"If I had failed to hit the apple and had killed my son, this one was for you. I promise

William Tell ready to prove his skill

you, I would not have failed to hit you."

When he heard this, Gessler roared with anger. He called the soldiers to bring his boat to shore.

"Put this man in chains," he shouted. "Throw him in the bottom of my boat. Take him to the other side of the lake. He is going to spend the rest of his life locked in my dungeon."

The soldiers struggled to get William chained securely. In spite of his strength, even William would not be able to escape from chains. The soldiers pushed him into the bottom of the boat. They laid William's bow next to him, since it would be safely out of William's reach. The villagers whispered among themselves. They did not like to see William Tell captured. Still, they were nervous and afraid of the soldiers. "Stand back!" shouted Gessler. "We are leaving."

Gessler stepped into the boat and told his soldiers to begin rowing. The soldiers pulled hard at the long oars, and the boat moved smoothly away from the shore.

When they were halfway across the lake, a sudden storm arose. Waves began to roll up and down. Lightning flashed again and again. The soldiers, who were mean and tough on land, were not good sailors. They were terrified when huge waves splashed into the boat.

"I cannot steer the boat," called one of the soldiers. "Let the prisoner loose. William is strong and knows the waters on this side of the lake."

"Nonsense," said Gessler angrily. "There is nothing to it. I will steer."

Gessler had trouble keeping the boat on course. It began spinning in circles. Just ahead was a group of large rocks. Gessler did not know if he could bring the boat safely around the rocks. He gave in and ordered the soldiers to take off William's chains.

"Sit here beside me and steer," shouted Gessler to William.

William picked up an oar and pulled just the right way. Very soon the boat stopped spinning and moved ahead. William brought the boat closer and closer to the rocks.

"Look out!" Gessler shouted to William. "We are going to hit!"

That was just what William had hoped to do. He pulled hard to the left, and the boat became lodged on a rock. William grabbed his bow and jumped out of the boat onto the rock. Then he turned, put his foot against the boat, and pushed it back into the water.

"Stop! What are you doing?" said Gessler.

It was too late. William leaped off the rock onto the shore. He hid among the trees and watched. The boat slid away from the rock and back into the stormy waves. The boat turned over. Gessler and the soldiers struggled through the waves to shore.

William knew they would be looking for him. He chose a tall tree and climbed up. There he waited quietly. Dripping and angry, Gessler led the soldiers on the search through the trees. When he got close to William's tree, William leaped down with his bow in his hand.

"There he is," shouted Gessler, pulling out a dagger and running toward William. William put his last arrow in the bow and then aimed, pulled, and released the arrow. William's aim was true. The arrow plunged into Gessler's heart, and he fell. When the soldiers saw that their leader was dead, they turned and ran.

Later that day, William returned to the village. Jem was overjoyed to see his father, safe and free.

News of Gessler's death soon spread throughout the village. Because of William's great courage, the villagers organized. They revolted against the tax collectors and against the king who had forced the taxes.

Neighboring villages joined William's village in the revolt. William Tell's bravery was a symbol to encourage all the people to become free. In time, there was a new free country—Switzerland.

William Tell is still a hero in Switzerland. Stories about him remind people of their freedom and of the bravery of their heroes.

1. *What did the people use to pay taxes?*
2. *What did Gessler make William Tell do when he brought him out of jail?*
3. *What happened to Gessler?*

The Boy Who Held Back the Sea

The Netherlands, once called Holland, is a country on the North Sea. Much of the land in this country is actually below the level of the sea. Water has been pumped out of the land to make dry land for people to live on and farm. Dikes have been built to keep the seawater out of the land. Dikes are well-packed walls of earth. Some water is directed into canals, and this water is used in the towns and on the farms. Along the dikes are gates that regulate the flow of water into canals. In this story, the boy's father is a gatekeeper for one of these gates.

Hans, a young boy of the Netherlands, lived in the city of Haarlem on the North Sea. One Saturday morning he awoke early. For the first time all week, the sun was shining.

"Ah, good," Hans said. "The holiday will not be spoiled. George and Jan will be waiting in the town square with ideas for new games."

He went down to breakfast.

"Good morning," his mother said. "I'm

glad to see you up so early. I have an errand for you."

"Today is my holiday," said Hans. "My friends are waiting for me."

"The errand will not take you long," said his mother. "Professor Muskens is not well. I have a fine round of cheese for him and also some of my red tulips. Even with his poor eyesight, the Professor should be able to see the bright color. That will please him."

Hans was about to object again. One look from his father silenced him. His father was a gatekeeper and did not get holidays at all. The gate Hans's father kept was a special kind. It slid up to let water from the sea flow into canals. The canals ran throughout the country, bringing water to the farms and villages. Boats used the canals every day to transport goods from town to town.

When enough water flowed in through the gate, Hans's father slammed the gate shut and locked it. Haarlem was several feet below the level of the sea. The gate was in a dike, a large wall built along the sea. If the gate was left open, seawater would rush in and flood the country.

Hans ate his breakfast slowly. When he finished, his mother gave him the cheese, the tulips, and his new blue jacket.

"Perhaps you can stay and read to the Professor," said his mother. "You can see your friends tomorrow."

Hans knew he had to go. He started off, dragging his feet. When Hans got near the town square, he could hear his friends there playing. He did not want them to see him because he felt a little silly carrying flowers and cheese. He turned into a side street. It led to the main road that went along beside the dike.

Hans walked on the road, out of sight of the town square. At the next curve there was a large bush. Hans, still unhappy about missing his friends, threw the flowers under the bush. When he reached a shady tree by the dike, he decided it was time to rest. He sat down near the tree and opened the cheese.

"This smells very good," said Hans. "I will take just a little bit of it."

Hans took one bite, then another and another. Soon the round of cheese was gone. Then Hans took off his jacket and rolled it into a pillow. He lay down and put it behind his head. He was quite comfortable.

Hans lay there by the tree for a long time.

He watched the turning arms of nearby windmills. He tried to count the clouds as they drifted by. He listened to the waves of the sea splash against the dike behind him. Then he fell asleep.

When Hans woke an hour later, he felt a trickle of water across his arm. He looked up. Although the sky was turning dark, it was not raining. He sat up and looked around. A thin stream of water was leaking through a hole in the dike near him.

Hans jumped to his feet. Like everyone who lived in the Netherlands, he understood the danger. If the water continued to leak, the small hole would soon be a large one. Water from the sea would pour through the hole. If it was not stopped, it would quickly become a flood. The fields of flowers, the town square, and his home would all be covered with water. Professor Muskens's cottage would also be flooded. The Professor, who was almost blind, would not even know the water was coming.

"Help!" Hans shouted, running back and forth along the dike.

He shouted again and again. There was no one nearby. Hans knew he must do something quickly. He ran back to the side of

Hans resting at the dike

the dike and then knelt beside the leak. He tried to patch it with mud, but the water still trickled through. Hans put a stone in the small hole, but the stone fell right out again. Then Hans pushed his thumb into the hole.

At last the water stopped. Hans sat down, keeping his thumb in the hole. Then he found he could lie down close to the dike and still keep the hole plugged. He continued to call out for help.

All afternoon, Hans lay next to the dike. No one heard his cries. No one came along the road.

At dusk, dark clouds rolled in and brought hard rain. Hans's shirt was soaked, and his shoes were covered with mud. Still he did not take his thumb out of the hole or move from the spot. Hans could hear the crashing waves on the other side of the dike. He wondered why his parents did not come to find him.

Hans's parents thought Hans had stayed with the professor because of the storm. They expected him home in the morning. So they locked the door and went to sleep.

Hans stayed pressed up against the side of the dike all through the long night. Sometimes his eyes would close, but he had to stay awake. His arm ached badly. Twice he almost gave up. He almost pulled his thumb out of the dike and let the sea run in. He did not, though. By morning there was a buzzing sound in his head. His legs were nearly numb, and his arms felt as if pins were sticking in them.

Just after dawn, a doctor was on his way home from visiting a sick child. The doctor noticed something red as he passed a bush by the crossroad. It was a bunch of tulips. That seemed strange. Then the doctor saw a blue bundle. He saw that it was a boy's jacket. The doctor looked beside the dike and saw a dirty, drooping figure. It was Hans.

Hans was very glad to see the doctor, but he hardly had the strength left to tell him so. The doctor took off his coat and wrapped it around Hans. Then he went for help.

Hans's father was the first to get to his son. He wiped the boy's face and gently pulled Han's thumb out of the dike. As workers repaired the leak, a sleeping Hans was carried home in his father's arms. Hans woke long enough to have a hot drink and a bath. Then he went to bed and slept all afternoon.

When Hans awoke, he found that he was

a hero. All his friends came to see him. Neighbors brought his favorite sweets. Even people he did not know came to thank him for saving the city.

Hans went into his mother's garden and cut both red and yellow tulips. He found his special book of adventure stories. Then he put on his second-best jacket. He tucked the book under one arm and the flowers under the other. Then he went to see his friend, Professor Muskens.

Hans spent the rest of the afternoon reading adventure stories to Professor Muskens. The best adventure story of all was not in the book, though. It was the adventure of Hans, who had held back the sea.

1. *Why did Hans not want to visit the professor?*
2. *Why was Haarlem's dike important?*
3. *How did Hans stop the leak?*

Reynard the Fox

Foxes have become known as clever or sly animals. This story is about a fox called Reynard who had a reputation for playing tricks on others. He always seemed to know the weaknesses of his friends and of his enemies.

The tales of Reynard the fox were first told in France. The stories were popular in other countries as well. They were especially well-known in Germany.

Reynard the fox had caused trouble all over the countryside. He had tricked almost all the animals, stealing their food and causing them all sorts of grief. Lion, king of the forest animals, declared that Reynard must answer for his bad deeds.

"Bring Reynard to me," King Lion said. "We will put him on trial. He will stand before our court and be judged."

The animals decided that Bear would find Reynard and bring him to court. Bear was eager to do this because he was among those who had suffered from the fox's pranks.

Bear set out for Reynard's home. He

walked all day, found a place to sleep at night, and then got up to walk again. After two days and two nights, Bear found Reynard's den.

"Hello, Reynard," he called. "It's Bear. Are you home?"

There was no answer. So he called again, "Reynard! Come on out and greet your old friend Bear."

Reynard heard Bear's rumbling voice, but he needed some time to think. He wanted to be ready to face an enemy as well as a friend.

Outside the den, Bear stood on one foot and then on another. He peered inside the opening, and he called again. He wondered if perhaps he had the wrong place.

At last, Reynard came to the front of his den. "Ah, Bear, it's you," he said. "I was just eating my lunch."

"Well, you must come with me to court," Bear said. "King Lion has sent for you. You are to stand trial because of your tricks."

Reynard knew that things were not likely to go well for him in court.

"Certainly, I will come," Reynard replied. "Just let me have my dessert first. You can join me, for I know where there is a huge honeycomb. If you will come with me, we can

Reynard answering Bear's call

both have some delicious honey."

Reynard did not really like honey, but he knew that Bear loved it. In fact, honey was Bear's favorite food.

"I believe I could enjoy some honey," Bear said. He was already smacking his lips. He was hungry from his long trip to find the fox.

Then Reynard and Bear walked to an old hollow tree. There was a hole in it about the size of Bear's head.

Reynard pointed and said, "Put your head in there. You'll find more honey than you've ever seen before."

Bear rushed to the tree. He peeked in but couldn't see any honey.

"It's deep in the tree," Reynard said. "You might have to reach far in."

Bear did that. He put both paws in the hole and then his whole head, too. Reynard helped by pushing on Bear's head.

"Enjoy yourself," said Reynard as he turned around to leave.

Bear didn't find the honey, but he found himself stuck in the tree!

Reynard smiled slyly. He walked off, leaving Bear struggling to get out of the tree.

"You're too greedy for your own good!" Reynard shouted back to Bear. Then he trotted home happily to plan more tricks to play on the animals.

1. *Why did King Lion send for Reynard?*
2. *What was Bear's favorite food?*
3. *Did Reynard help Bear by pushing on his head? Why or why not?*

The Lark and the Wolf

A lark is a small songbird common in Europe. This story from Poland tells of a lark and a wolf who become friends. In many stories from Europe, the wolf is a vicious creature. In this story, however, the wolf is helpful.

At sunrise the lark began to sing her song of happiness. She was happy because the fields were green, the sun was warm, and she had five new babies. The babies were snug in their nest. The nest was in a low red and brown bush at the edge of the forest. A stream flowed gently not far away.

As the lark sang, she looked all around at the bush and the trees and then at the ground. She was satisfied that all was well until she saw something strange. In the field close by, the ground was moving! She stopped her singing and flew over to see what was happening.

The trembling ground opened into a hole, and a mole poked his head out.

The lark, afraid for her babies, asked, "What are you doing?"

"You cannot know much of the world," the

mole said without even looking up. "I am a mole. Moles dig burrows. I am digging my burrow. Now please don't ask me any more questions."

The lark had to ask again. "I see that you are digging. Where is your burrow going?"

"I'm resting just now," said the mole. "Soon I will dig toward that red and brown bush at the edge of the forest."

"Oh please, dig someplace else," the lark wailed. "My babies are in that bush. If you dig under it, my babies will fall out of their nest and die. They are far too young to fly. You have a whole field to dig in."

"That's too bad," the mole said. "I like that brown and red bush."

The lark ruffled her feathers and tried to seem fierce. "I will peck your head until you bleed," she said.

"I have a hard head," the mole replied. "Go right ahead. You will probably break your beak."

"Please have pity on my young ones," the lark begged.

"If you don't like where I'm going, move somewhere else and build a new nest," the mole said. Then he shrugged his shoulders and ducked back into the hole.

The lark gave up and flew off for help. She looked for someone who was bigger than a mole. The lark reached a nearby farm where she heard dogs barking. She thought she would ask the dogs for help. Dogs were good at chasing things. She chirped trying to get the dogs' attention. The barking dogs were chasing the pigs. Between the barking of the dogs and the squealing of the pigs, she couldn't make herself heard.

She flew on toward the farmhouse. Near it, a large cat slept on the mat near the front door. The lark considered asking the cat for help. The cat looked up with interest as the lark hovered near. Then the cat stood up and stretched, ready for action. The lark knew how delicious young birds tasted to cats. She decided she wouldn't ask for the cat's help and so flew on by.

As the lark soared away in haste, she almost hit the barn. She recovered and looked down to see that a large rooster was busy stuffing himself with grain. Here was someone big enough and tough enough to tackle a mole.

The lark made a lot of noise to get the rooster's attention. She called out as loud as she could, "Chirp! Trouble! Chirp! Trouble!"

The sound echoed throughout the barn. The rooster thought it was the farmer coming to beat him for taking the grain. He raced out the door and away as fast as he could.

The lark had to look elsewhere. She saw some fine large geese. The geese were so busy eating in the orchard that they would not help. She saw a small quail. The quail was having so much fun playing with a leaf that she would not listen.

It was getting late. The lark wondered how long it would take the mole to reach the red and brown bush. She flew into the woods to think but couldn't come up with a way to help her babies. She perched on a tree and began to cry loudly.

A wolf was napping beside a log under that tree. The lark's cries woke him. He came out angry and grumbling.

"Why are you making such noise?" the wolf asked. "Don't you know that respectable animals nap in the afternoon? Go away and let me sleep."

"Oh, my friend," the lark said. "I am in such trouble. I have tried to find help but I can't find any. There is nothing left for me to do but cry."

The wolf had never been called "friend" by a bird before. He rather liked the sound of it.

"Perhaps, just perhaps, I can help," the wolf said. "I make no promises. What is your terrible trouble?"

The lark told him about the mole who was digging near her babies' nest. The wolf really didn't care much about the baby birds. He did like the idea of a little excitement. "Well," the clever wolf said, "I might help you. I am far too hungry to work, though."

The lark, encouraged by the friendly response, said, "I will find food for you."

"You are a tiny bird," the wolf said. "You cannot even pick up a meat pie. Even so, I'll let you show me what you can do. Let's see whether you can find food for me."

The wolf followed as the lark circled around the surrounding fields. As she flew over the fields, she saw a place where there was plenty of food.

A wedding had just taken place. Friends had prepared a large party for the happy couple. In the small cabin were tables filled with large platters of food. There was far too much food for all of the people at the party.

The lark flew down to the wolf and told him about the party and the food.

"Stand by and await your chance," the lark said confidently.

She flew into the cabin and circled around. She flapped her wings slowly and flew down close to the table. She flew back up and then down again, almost dipping into a platter. Up and down she flew. She would get close to the guests and then zoom away. The wedding guests would jump up and try each time to catch her. When the lark saw that all the guests were on their feet, she flew out the door.

The guests followed the lark outside. While the lark flew just out of the guests' reach, the wolf climbed in the cabin window.

The wolf ate five sausages, three dumplings, half a pie, and a huge slice of tender meat. He was so full he could hardly pull himself back out the window. He did manage to just get out before the guests returned.

When the lark saw that the wolf was safely out of sight, she flew straight up and away. She did not wait to see what happened when the guests went back into the cabin.

"Now, come and help my babies," the lark said to the wolf.

"I am very thirsty," the wolf said. "I could

work much better if I had something to drink."

"There is a stream right here close to my nest," the lark said.

"No, no, not water. Something more interesting," the wolf requested.

The anxious mother replied, "All right, I'll see what I can find. Come along with me. I'll fly above you and let you know when I find 'something interesting'."

The lark flew along the road from the forest toward the town. As she flew, she saw the innkeeper and his son driving along in a wagon. They were taking barrels of wine to the wedding.

"Hide in the ditch," the lark called to the wolf below. "Watch what happens and come out when I call you."

Then she flew down and sat on the front of the wagon. The innkeeper's hand slowly crept out. It was good luck to catch a lark. The lark jumped quickly onto a barrel. The innkeeper took off his hat and tried to throw it over the lark. The lark, enjoying herself, flew up and landed on the innkeeper's head.

"Stay still," the innkeeper's son said. "I will catch the lark." He got out of the wagon and picked up a stone.

The bird flew off the innkeeper's head and onto his whip. In a flash she went from the whip to the wagon seat and then to a barrel. The boy threw his stone at the lark. It missed the bird but hit the barrel. A trickle of wine began running out of the barrel.

The innkeeper got out of the wagon to look at the barrel. He was in a rage when he saw his precious wine leaking out. He yelled at his son, "Now look what you've done!"

The son started running as fast as he could back down the road. The innkeeper ran after him.

As soon as the innkeeper and his son were out of sight, the lark called to the wolf. He leapt up on the wagon. He put his tongue out and lapped up the wine as it trickled out. He drank until he could drink no more. Then he stumbled down from the wagon and went into the woods.

The lark flew up to him.

"Have you had enough food and drink?" she asked.

"Oh, yes I have," groaned the wolf. "You have done your part very well, and now I will do mine."

They went back to the red and brown bush. The lark's nest and her babies were still there, but the ground nearby was quivering. The lark and the wolf had arrived just in time.

The wolf sat by the moving earth and waited. When the mole came up for air, the wolf grabbed him. First he shook him a bit. Then he took him off to a field on the other side of the forest and left him. The mole never came near the lark's nest again.

"Now you shall have peace," the wolf said, "and so will I." He went back to the log where he had been napping before the lark asked for help. He closed his eyes.

The lark left her nest and flew slowly around the wolf's resting place. She said softly, "Thank you, my friend."

The wolf slowly opened one eye and looked at the lark.

"It was a pleasure, my friend," he said. He grinned as he thought of all the good food and drink.

The lark went back to her nest to tend to her children. The field was peaceful once again. The lark could sing her song of happiness. She would always keep a watch for another mole. She hoped that she could always count on the wolf, her new friend.

1. *Where was the lark's nest?*
2. *Why didn't the lark ask the cat to help her?*
3. *What did the lark get the wolf to eat?*

Dinner in the Woods

This story is from the Ukraine. Many Ukrainian stories are told to make people laugh and also to teach lessons. In this story some forest animals are persuaded to believe a rumor. The humorous results show that rumors aren't always true.

Fox had lived in the woods for a long time. She knew where the birds nested and where all sorts of other forest animals lived. She knew where the freshest water flowed. She knew her woods, but she had never been to the village nearby.

One spring day, Fox decided to leave her den and stroll to the village. She wanted to see what it was like. Just as she reached the first building in the village, its door burst open. Out flew a screeching creature covered with silky black fur. Fox jumped back. The creature landed just in front of her.

"I have lived in the woods for a long time," said Fox. "I have never seen an animal like you. Who are you?"

The cat (for that is what it was) drew himself up straight.

"I am Pan Kotsky," he said. "I am the most frightful animal in the world. I rip and tear to pieces anyone I please."

Fox thought it would be a good idea to become friends with this ferocious animal.

"I have quite a nice home in the woods," said Fox. "Would you come with me for a visit?"

When Pan Kotsky agreed to come, Fox proudly showed the way to her home. Pan Kotsky made himself comfortable and decided to stay a while. Fox did everything she could to please Pan Kotsky. Fox brought food, and the cat ate it all. She gave him the best place in the den to sleep. For several days Pan Kotsky did not leave Fox's den.

Other animals in the forest became curious about Fox's new guest. One day Rabbit met Fox.

"Hello, Cousin Fox," said Rabbit. "I was just on my way to pay you a visit."

"No!" said Fox. "Do not come. Pan Kotsky is staying with me, and he will tear you to pieces."

Rabbit told Wolf about Pan Kotsky. Wolf told Bear, and Bear told Wild Boar. They were all very curious about this creature, but they were also a bit afraid. They tried to think of a way to see Pan Kotsky without being seen themselves.

"Pan Kotsky seems to like good food," said Rabbit. "Let's cook a fine dinner and invite Fox and her new friend." They all agreed and tried to think of the most tempting meal.

Wolf had an idea. His favorite meal was borscht, a delicious beet soup.

"Borscht," said Wolf. "There is nothing as tasty as a pot of good borscht."

"Good," said Wild Boar. "I will dig up some beets."

"I will bring some potatoes to put in the soup," said Wolf.

"There should be some cabbage left in my yard," Rabbit said. "I will bring a few tender leaves."

"I have a bit of honeycomb put aside," Bear said. "That would be a nice sweet for dessert."

At that, the animals all went off to gather their food.

After they came back, the animals built a fire and began to get ready for their dinner. Wolf pulled his big pot out of its winter storage place. Bear went to the stream and filled it with water. Wild Boar hung the pot on a large branch over the fire.

While the borscht cooked, the animals tried to decide who would invite Pan Kotsky.

"I am much too slow to go," said Bear. "If Pan Kotsky decides to chase me, I could never get away."

"I am just as slow as you are," said Wild Boar, as if it were an honor.

Wolf made his voice shake a little. He said, "I am really very old and I do not see very well."

That left only Rabbit to take Pan Kotsky the invitation to dinner. He ran to Fox's den and hopped about outside the entrance. Fox saw him and came out.

"Why are you here?" she asked.

"The animals wish to honor your new friend. I have come here to invite you and Pan Kotsky for dinner," said Rabbit. He added a polite twitch of his nose.

Fox thought for a bit.

"Yes," she said. "We will come. You must all hide, however, or Pan Kotsky will tear you to pieces."

Quickly, Rabbit ran back with the news.

"Yes, yes, they are coming. Fox said we must hide. If he sees us, Pan Kotsky will tear us to pieces."

No one wanted such a thing to happen,

but they did want to see this fearful creature. Wild Boar placed the steaming dinner on the table. Then he squeezed under the table. He managed to hide all of himself but the very tip of his tail. Bear climbed up into an oak tree and hid in the branches. Wolf and Rabbit hid behind a big log.

Soon Fox and the creature arrived. Fox led the cat right up to the table. When Pan Kotsky saw the food, he leapt right up and began to eat. He ate very quickly, purring "mmmor" over and over.

To the animals in hiding, it sounded like "More." They were astonished. How could a small creature eat all they had prepared and still want more?

When Pan Kotsky had eaten all he could hold, he stretched out on the table.

A bug bit the tip of Wild Boar's tail, which was sticking out from under the table. Wild Boar flicked it off. Pan Kotsky thought the tail was a mouse. He leapt from the table and grabbed the tail with his sharp claws.

Wild Boar leapt up, thinking he was about to be torn to pieces. Wild Boar was so frightened he knocked over the table. Then he charged into the oak tree where Bear was hiding.

Bear jumped from the tree, thinking he was about to be torn to pieces. Wild Boar crashed into the log where Wolf and Rabbit were hiding.

Wolf and Rabbit, thinking they were about to be torn to pieces, jumped out from behind the log.

The animals ran off in four different directions.

Pan Kotsky was startled by all this noise. Who was after him? What was it? He ran to the oak tree and climbed to safety.

Much later that night Wolf, Bear, and Wild Boar gathered. They began to talk about the dinner.

Wild Boar had not yet fully recovered. "He grabbed me by the tail and threw me against the oak tree," he said, panting.

"He grabbed my hide and threw me right out of the oak tree," said Bear.

Wolf, limping along, joined them. "He picked up that big log and hit me across the back. I can hardly walk," he said.

Rabbit never did come back.

Pan Kotsky, that frightful creature, sat shaking in the oak tree all night. He may be there yet.

Pan Kotsky and friends

1. *What did the animals cook for Pan Kotsky's dinner?*
2. *Who invited Pan Kotsky to dinner?*
3. *What caused Pan Kotsky to bite Wild Boar's tail?*

The Beautiful Rose

This story is from France. It is also called "Beauty and the Beast." The main character in the story is named Belle-Rose. In French, her name means "beautiful rose."

Three Gifts

Long ago there was a French merchant named René. His three daughters, Nicole, Michelle, and Belle-Rose were the great joy of his life.

One snowy winter morning, René was preparing to go to the city. Before leaving, he asked each daughter what gift she wanted. He would bring gifts as well as the goods they needed.

Nicole, who was selfish, answered first. "Bring me a dress made of silk," she said.

Michelle, who wanted whatever her sister wanted, only more, answered next. She said, "I want a dress made of silk and also gold!"

Belle-Rose listened quietly.

"What do you want, Belle-Rose?" her father asked.

She thought for a moment. She really had

everything she needed. At last, she answered, "I would like a rose."

"A rose you shall have," her father said. He loaded his wagon and hitched up the horses. Then he rode off to the city.

René found the dresses for Nicole and Michelle. When his youngest daughter asked for a rose, he had not thought it would be difficult to find. Now he realized that since it was winter, there would not be roses blooming. No one in the city had roses. So he left without Belle's rose.

On his way home, René was surprised to see a beautiful rosebush in full bloom. It was growing by a fence on the grounds of an old castle. Although there was snow outside the fence, there was no snow on the castle grounds.

"Why has the snow not covered this place?" René wondered. "How can the roses be blooming in this winter weather? Perhaps this place is magic. Whatever the reason, I am very glad to see it. I will be able to take Belle her rose after all."

He got out of the wagon, climbed over the fence, and plucked the flower.

At once, he heard a startling noise. He turned around to see that a huge, furry creature had come up behind him.

The Beast said with a loud growl, "Why have you taken my flower? Anyone who steals my flowers may pay with his life."

René was terrified and fell to his knees. "Don't kill me, Beast," he said. "I've only picked one rose for my daughter, Belle-Rose."

The Beast's voice became softer. "Belle-Rose?" he said. "Tell me about her."

René said that his daughter was a kind and gentle person. He explained that she was as beautiful as she was kind.

The Beast listened. Then he said, "Bring her to me. I will spare your life if Belle-Rose willingly comes in your place. If she will not come, then you must come back and pay the price."

The Beast gave René one week to return or to send Belle-Rose. René was too scared to think of what to do other than to accept the Beast's offer.

"Don't fail me," the Beast called as René got back into his wagon. René rode home shaking with fear.

When René arrived home, he presented his daughters with their gifts. Nicole and Michelle ran off to try on their dresses. Belle held her rose but looked worried.

"What is wrong, Father?" she asked. "Has bringing these gifts made you unhappy?"

"No, my daughter," he said. "I have had a frightening adventure. I must talk to you and your sisters about it."

When the older two returned in their silken gowns, René told his daughters what had happened. He told them where the castle was. He told about the Beast who was so angry because of the rose.

Nicole and Michelle agreed that Belle-Rose should go to the old castle.

"They're right, Father," Belle-Rose said bravely. "I will go and face the Beast."

"No, no," René said. "You shall not go. None of my daughters will go. I will return myself."

Belle did not want her father to go. She felt sure he would be killed.

Belle Meets Beast

That night, Belle-Rose took one of the horses from the stable and rode into the woods. The horse needed little direction from Belle-Rose. It headed straight to the castle.

When Belle-Rose got to the palace, she saw that it was dark and cold looking. There were lights on inside the castle, though.

Belle-Rose got off her horse and peered into the window. The room looked warm, and a table was set with a grand feast. The Beast sat at the head of the table.

Belle was frightened at the sight of the Beast, but she knew she must face him anyway.

The Beast looked up and saw the young woman at the window. He went to the door and called to her. He could tell by her beauty that she must be Belle-Rose.

"Won't you come and eat with me, Belle-Rose?" the Beast asked. Belle was surprised at the gentleness in his voice.

"Aren't you going to kill me?" she asked timidly.

"No!" the Beast shouted. This idea seemed to have made him angry. Then he calmed down a little. "I could never harm you," he said.

Belle-Rose went in and sat at the table where they ate in silence.

The Beast explained to Belle-Rose where she would sleep. Before she went to her room, he said, "You are so very beautiful. Will you marry me?"

The girl was shocked. "I must be truthful, Beast," she said. "I cannot marry you, for you

Belle-Rose at the Beast's castle

are much too frightening to look at."

Twenty-nine days and nights passed. The Beast always saw to it that Belle-Rose had everything she needed and everything she wanted. They slowly began to trust each other. They read poetry together. In the evenings they walked in the garden and watched the starry sky.

Each night the Beast asked Belle-Rose to marry him. Each night she could only answer no.

On the thirtieth day, Belle-Rose and the Beast were walking together in the garden. Belle-Rose decided to ask the Beast for a favor.

"You have been very kind to me," she began. "Will you please let me go home? I dreamed that my father was very ill. I would like to visit him. I would stay only a short while."

The Beast knew that Belle-Rose might not return. By this time, though, his love for her was great. It was impossible for him to refuse her request.

"You may go," he said. "If you do not come back in ten days, though, I will surely die of grief."

Then the Beast gave Belle-Rose a

wonderful magic ring. The ring made it possible for her to go back home in a mere moment.

Belle-Rose's Decision

Belle-Rose reached her home safely. Her father was overjoyed that she was still alive and that she looked so well. Her sisters were curious about her life at the castle.

"I can stay only ten days," she explained.

Nicole asked, "If you don't go back, will the Beast come and kill us?"

"Oh no," answered Belle-Rose. "The Beast is kind and gentle. He would never hurt anyone. If I don't go back, he will die of grief."

This did not concern Nicole and Michelle. Besides, they were jealous of their sister's new life.

Soon the ten days had passed, and it was time for Belle-Rose to go back to the Beast. The older sisters found a way to hide the number of days from Belle-Rose.

Two weeks passed before Belle-Rose realized that she had been gone so long. She also realized that she missed the Beast. She wanted to go back.

She gathered her things and said good-bye to her family. She used the magic ring to get back to the Beast's home.

When she reached the castle, Belle-Rose saw that there were no lights. The castle looked as cold inside as it was outside. The flowers had wilted, and snow covered the grounds.

Belle-Rose looked all around for the Beast. At last, she found him in the garden. He was huddled in a corner and was barely breathing.

She ran to him and spoke. "Oh, Beast!" she said. "What has happened to you?"

"Belle-Rose," he whispered because he was so weak. "Will you marry me?"

She held his head in her arms. "Don't die, my love," she said. "Yes, I will proudly be your wife."

The Beast was quiet. Belle-Rose thought she was too late to save him. Her tears fell on his fur.

Then a remarkable thing happened. Belle-Rose's tears brought life back into the Beast and also changed him into a handsome prince.

The prince explained that he had been under a spell. Belle-Rose's love had broken the spell and her tears had been the sign of her true love.

Belle-Rose and the prince were married. They always kept rosebushes growing at the entrance to the castle.

On their dinner table in the evening there was always one beautiful rose.

1. *Why couldn't Belle-Rose's father find a rose in the city?*
2. *What did the Beast want as payment for the rose?*
3. *Why did the Beast nearly die?*

The Song of the Lorelei

In German myths, the Rhine River was known as Father Rhine. Father Rhine had daughters who were water maidens, or nymphs. One of Father Rhine's daughters was the Lorelei. She was a beautiful but heartless maiden who sang a dangerous song each night.

The Danger of the Lorelei

All day long the Lorelei slept in the cool water at the bottom of the Rhine. At night, she would awaken to spend the moonlight hours singing and combing her long lovely hair. She would rise from the river and climb the tall cliff at the water's edge. At the top of the cliff, she would sit down and look out over the dark blue-green water.

Each night the Lorelei would take out a comb that sparkled in the moonlight. Then she would begin to comb her golden hair. As she combed the water from her hair, the Lorelei would sing a beautiful song. The sound of her singing would float from the high rock and would echo along the river. Sometimes sailors on the Rhine River would hear the music. The songs were so beautiful that the sailors would forget what they were supposed to do. They would forget where they were going, and they would forget to steer their boats. Their boats would run into the cliff and break into pieces. Many sailors died after falling under the spell of the Lorelei's song. The Lorelei did not care about the sailors. She would just laugh softly as the sailors sank forever into the river.

One young man who drowned because of hearing the Lorelei's song was the son of Prince Palatine. The saddened prince became very angry about the Lorelei's singing. "Someone must find the beautiful singer," he said. "We must find a way to make her drown, as my son was drowned."

Prince Palatine thought that many of his subjects would be willing to help get rid of the Lorelei. He discovered, though, that only one man was willing to try. This man was Diether, a captain in the prince's army. Eventually, Diether was able to persuade a band of soldiers to help destroy the Lorelei.

The Soldiers' Attempt

Diether and his soldiers started down the river by day, when the Lorelei would be sleeping. At sunset they reached the place where so many sailors had died. Then they quietly climbed up the tall, rocky cliff.

"Spread out," Diether told his soldiers. "We must not let the Lorelei climb down and escape. We will drown her in the river just as she has drowned our prince's son."

Then, just as the moon began to rise, the soldiers saw her.

"Look at the top of the cliff," said one of the men. "There is the Lorelei getting ready to cause boat wrecks. See how she calmly braids jewels into her long wet hair."

At that, the Lorelei turned and saw the soldiers. She was not afraid, and she looked directly at them. The soldiers looked deep into the Lorelei's beautiful eyes. At that moment, a spell fell on the men. They could not move, and they could not talk. They could only watch. The Lorelei laughed as she took the jewels from her hair and threw them into the water. Then she called upon her father.

"Father Rhine, I send you my jewels. I ask you to bring me a way to escape these soldiers."

As the jewels fell into the water, a wild storm arose. The waves of the Rhine became

The Lorelei escaping

higher and higher until they reached the top of the cliff.

Suddenly, out of the great foamy waves, came three white horses with white foamy manes. The horses pulled a chariot that was as blue-green as the river. The Lorelei looked once more at the soldiers. Then she stepped into the chariot and took the horses' reins. She drove the chariot straight into the raging storm on the river. In the middle of the river, the Lorelei and the chariot sank from sight.

When the chariot disappeared, the storm stopped. The river grew quiet, and the soldiers were released from their spell. Diether then called them together to return to Prince Palatine and report what had happened.

The Lorelei was never seen again. However, late at night, travelers on the Rhine still say they can hear her beautiful singing. From the place where she used to sit, the wind seems to carry echoes of her songs. Sometimes, too, there are boat wrecks at that rocky spot where sailors still fall under the Lorelei's spell.

1. *Where did the Lorelei go at night?*
2. *Why did Prince Palatine become angry with the Lorelei?*
3. *How did the Lorelei escape Diether and his soldiers?*

The Secret of Mélusine

This love story was most likely first told in the Middle Ages in a rural part of France.

Raymond's Good Luck

Raymond of Poitou was a knight in the service of his brother, the Count of Forez. Raymond's older brother had inherited the family's wealth. Even though Raymond was less fortunate than his brother in land and money, he was nonetheless happy. In fact, he was happier than his wealthy brother. For all his money, the Count of Forez had a disagreeable nature.

One afternoon Raymond, along with his servants, went hunting. They were on the property of his cousin, the Count of Poitier. Following a deer, Raymond led his horse along a path away from the servants. He killed the deer, but he got lost. The servants returned to the count's court, but Raymond wandered through the forest.

As night fell, Raymond, tired and thirsty, stopped by a bubbling spring in a clearing. He got down off the horse for a drink from the spring. As he bent down to the water, Raymond heard a voice behind him.

"Hello," said the voice.

Raymond swiftly rose and turned with his blade drawn in case the person were dangerous. Instead, he saw a beautiful young woman. He tried to speak but could only stumble on words.

"Who . . . who . . . ?" he tried.

"I am Mélusine," she said.

Raymond had never before seen such a lovely woman. He tried to introduce himself, "I am . . ."

"You are Raymond, a knight from Poitou," Mélusine said.

"How did you know that?"

"I know a lot of things," Mélusine said with a mysterious smile.

"Then you know that I am a poor knight," Raymond said. "You must also know that at this moment I wish I had lands and riches. If I did, I would ask you to marry me this night."

Mélusine said, "Your cousin, the Count of Poitier, loves you dearly. He would give you land if you would ask."

"You could be right," said Raymond.

"Leave your deer here, and return to your

cousin," Mélusine said. "Ask to have this spring. Then ask for as much land around the spring as can be covered by the deer's skin. After that, hurry back to me. I will be waiting here."

Raymond rode through the forest as if in a dream. He thought about what Mélusine asked and considered it strange. However, he was already so deeply in love that he trusted the woman completely.

Raymond found his way back to the castle of his cousin. He went to the count and made his request.

"My lord," he said to Count Poitier. "You know I have few possessions of my own. I ask that you grant me a spring I have seen in the forest of Coulombiers. I also ask for as much land around the spring as can be covered by a deer's skin."

"That seems a small and reasonable request," the count said.

His wish granted, Raymond and his servants returned to the forest. Raymond showed the way to the spring. Mélusine was waiting there, as she had promised.

"The spring is mine," the knight reported.

"Then have your servants skin the deer," Mélusine said.

After this was done, the woman directed the servants to cut the skin into thin strips. Then Mélusine took the strips and tied them into a long rope. After that, she had them stretch the rope around a large area of ground.

Raymond saw that this was a clever idea. He would get quite a bit of land this way. With the land he gained that day, he was not poor anymore!

At the end of the day, Raymond again declared his love for this unusual woman.

"Mélusine," he said, "I offer you my lands and my heart. Will you marry me?"

"Yes," she answered, "but only under one condition. You must never follow me or ask what I have done."

Raymond agreed without hesitation.

Raymond's Mistake

Mélusine and Raymond were married. They were blessed with happiness from the first day of their marriage.

A great castle was built with the help of Mélusine. She used a mouthful of water and a handful of stones. Although Raymond thought this, too, was strange, he did not question his wife.

They named the castle Lusignan. The land was quite rich and provided crops every season without fail.

Every Saturday Mélusine would leave Raymond. She always returned by early the next morning. Raymond never asked where she went, and he never followed her.

Raymond and Mélusine had ten sons. Each was as mysterious as he was unique. Guy, the oldest son, had one green eye and one red. Reanault had only one eye, but he could see for more than fifty miles. Geoffrey, the bravest son, had the nose of a wild boar. Even Phillipe, the best-looking son, had a huge wart on his nose.

Raymond's older brother had not come to visit in all the time Raymond and Mélusine had been married. Twelve years after the marriage, the count came to see Raymond on a Saturday. Raymond greeted his brother with great joy.

The Count of Forez had never understood how his younger brother had been so favored. He was jealous of Raymond's happiness and began to raise questions.

"Where is Mélusine, my beautiful sister-in-law?" he asked.

"I never see her on Saturdays," Raymond

said. "She is always away as she is today."

"That's strange," the count said. "Is there any reason for that?"

"No. It's what she wishes."

"Have you ever wondered where she's gone?" the count asked. "Have you ever wondered why she gives birth to children who aren't normal? Maybe she's a witch or in league with the devil. She could come to harm you, my brother."

Raymond was upset and impatient with his brother. He said, "Mélusine and my children are the most wonderful people in my life. She would certainly never harm me or our children."

Although Raymond had defended his wife, he was bothered by his brother's words. He began to doubt Mélusine for the first time. After the count left, he went out to find his wife.

Raymond knew that Mélusine locked herself in a tower on Saturdays. He went to the tower and tried the door. It was locked, so he looked through the keyhole.

He saw Mélusine combing her hair. He also saw that the lower half of her body was a serpent.

Raymond screamed in horror at what he

Mélusine

saw. Mélusine heard him. As she turned toward him, she gave a great shriek.

"I can never again be with you!" she cried. "You were never to follow me. Now I must go away from you and never return."

With that, she disappeared from sight.

Raymond had not kept his part of their agreement. He went home sadly to tell his sons what had happened. They never saw Mélusine again.

Raymond lived on with his sons, who all grew up to be respected and wealthy.

What Raymond had not known was that Mélusine was a magical creature. She could live as any other woman all the time except on Saturdays. On Saturdays, she turned into a half-serpent that must not be seen by any human. After she was seen that day, she had to keep the shape of a serpent. She would be immortal as a serpent, however.

Mélusine's spirit never left Lusignan. Whenever there was danger, her warning shrieks could be heard throughout the castle.

1. Who gave Raymond the land around
   the spring?
2. What did Mélusine use to help build
   the castle?
3. What happened to Mélusine when
   Raymond saw her?

Till Feeds the Town

Stories of Till Eulenspiegel, the prankster, are told in many countries. They began in northern Germany in the Middle Ages but were told in many other places as well. There are more than 40 tales about Till. This one comes from Germany. It finds Till in a country that became the Netherlands.

Till is a young man who is always playing tricks. Sometimes the tricks have very good results, as they do here.

This story includes a man called a burgomaster. The burgomaster was the chief magistrate, or the mayor.

"KABOOM!"

A cannonball exploded in the middle of Sterkdam. Then came another and yet another. The city of Sterkdam was under attack. Since late in October a thousand Spanish solidiers had kept Sterkdam under siege. Every day their battery of twelve heavy cannons fired on Sterkdam.

Sterkdam was surrounded by a wall that

had several iron gates. These gates were guarded by townspeople who controlled who came in and out of the city. They could not control the cannonballs that came over the top, though.

Inside the walled city, the people wept. It was December 24, and snow lay on the ground. The people in the city were cold, hungry, and depressed. Everyone from the burgomaster to the one prisoner in jail was suffering.

Till, the one prisoner, had stolen a pair of shoes early in the siege. He stole the shoes knowing he would go to jail. There he would at least have a warm place to sleep and some food to eat.

The food had run out, though, and now Till was cold, hungry, and restless. It was Christmas Eve. Till needed to think of a way to get out of jail.

Till stood by the barred window staring out. In the street outside he saw a young boy holding his stomach and crying.

"What's the matter with you?" Till asked.

"I'm so hungry," the boy wailed. "Not even St. Nicholas will be able to break through the Spanish lines."

Till was a mischief-maker and sometimes

a thief, but he tried to help people when he could.

"Go and fetch me a bucket of blue paint and a brush," he said.

"What?" the boy asked curiously.

"Yes, get a bucket of blue paint," Till said. "It must be light blue like the sky. Get a brush, too. Hurry!" Till said all this under his breath so that the guards would not be able to hear him.

The boy rushed away. Soon he returned with the paint and the brush. Till tied the sheets from his bed into knots to make a rope. Then he lowered it to the boy.

"Now tie that end to the bucket," Till said.

Till raised the bucket to the window. He then dipped the brush in the bucket and painted the bars with the sky blue paint. Next, he lowered the bucket back down to the boy.

"Now please take the bucket and the brush away. Don't tell anyone about any of this," Till warned.

"Why not? What are you trying to do?" the boy asked.

"Just wait," Till said, and he winked. "St. Nicholas with his presents just might make his way to Sterkdam tonight."

The boy's eyes widened, and a smile brightened his dusty face. He dashed off.

Till screamed loud enough for the guards to hear him. "Good-bye! Oh, and thanks for letting me visit!"

Till dived under his bed. When the guards came in, they looked at the window. Since the bars had been painted to look the same as the sky outside, they couldn't be seen. It looked to the guards as though the bars had disappeared.

"Till has escaped!" they shouted. Then the guards left the cell without locking the gate.

Till grabbed his bed sheet and escaped from his cell with no problem. He ran right away toward the gates of the city.

Till headed for the nearest gate. There stood a man with a musket. Till knew that the orders were to let no one in or out. He opened up the white sheet and draped it over his head. Then he walked toward the gate.

The guard took one look at Till and said, "It's a ghost!"

Then the guard said in a trembling voice, "What do you want?"

"I want you to let me through the gate," Till said in a ghostly voice.

The guard seemed curious. "Shouldn't you

be able to go through the wall if you are a ghost?" he asked.

"Be silent and do as I say—or else!" Till warned the guard.

The guard quickly let Till through the gate without further delay.

Till's plan was simple: While draped in the sheet, he was invisible in the snow. He ran out of the town and made his way over to the Spanish camp. He sneaked into the camp and began to look around.

The Spanish soldiers were preparing for a big Christmas Eve feast. There was food everywhere.

Till was able to get into an empty tent. There he found a Spanish uniform, which he put on, and two large sacks, which he took. Then he slowly moved out among the Spanish soldiers.

Till began to gather food from around the fires and in the tents.

"Where are you going with that food?" one of the soldiers asked.

"It's for the General," Till answered, giving a big salute.

Till loaded the sacks with chicken, geese, and strings of sausages. He packed in breads, nuts, cheeses, and pastries. Till's biggest steal was a large Christmas pudding.

As darkness fell, the soldiers began to feast. They left their posts at the cannons. Till silently went up to the cannon battery. There he removed the cannonballs from all of the twelve cannons. Then he stuffed the barrels full of the food he had stolen.

After Till stuffed all twelve cannons with food, he went to look for the artillery captain. The captain was sitting under a tree relaxing after his dinner.

Till saluted and said, "Sir, the General sends orders. He wants you and your men to fire a single volley at midnight."

"At midnight?" the captain said. "It will be dark. How will we be able to aim if we cannot see to fix our sights?"

"That's my problem," Till said. "I am going to sneak into the town and light a torch in the church bell tower."

"That's very dangerous. You are a brave young man."

"Be ready for my signal, sir," Till said. Then he hurried out of the camp and back to Sterkdam.

There was a windmill close to the Sterkdam city wall. By catching one of the windmill blades, Till got up to the top of the

Till loading the cannons

wall. From there he jumped down into the streets of the town.

The streets of Sterkdam were nearly deserted. Most people had gone to bed early because of hunger. Only a handful of guards stood watch. They were tired and hungry and didn't take notice of Till. At this point, Till made his way to the top of the bell tower.

"Wake up!" Till shouted at the top of his lungs. "Wake up! St. Nicholas is coming!"

Doors flew open, and shutters were raised. Men dressed in nightshirts ran to the streets with their muskets. Women clung to their children. The guards who were still awake rushed to see Till waving excitedly over them.

"That's Till the thief!" the burgomaster cried. "He escaped from prison just this afternoon. Seize him!"

Till lit a torch and began waving it.

"He's gone mad!" the burgomaster screamed. "He's signaling the Spaniards!"

The Spanish artillery captain saw the torch, too. He understood it was the signal for him to fire.

"All batteries fire!" he commanded.

A thunderous burst came from the artillery battery. It could be heard from miles around. Everyone in Sterkdam scrambled for cover. Everyone, that is, but for Till. He caught a cooked goose that was shot from a Spanish cannon.

Ducks, chickens, hams, sausages, fruit, cakes, nuts, cheeses, and breads all fell out of the sky like rain. For the first time in months, the people of Sterkdam smiled.

"I told you St. Nicholas was coming," Till said with a hearty laugh.

The town celebrated all night long. Their hunger had passed, and their spirits were raised. After Till explained what had happened, he was given an official pardon and made the guest of honor.

Early on Christmas morning, an army of soldiers from the Netherlands came to the rescue of Sterkdam. They drove the army away and freed the besieged city.

Till, who had begun the day as a common thief, became a hero. The people of Sterkdam erected a bronze statue of Till that read:

Till Eulenspiegel:
The thief who stole Christmas

1. *Why couldn't the prison guards see the prison bars?*
2. *Why did Till take the cannonballs out of the Spanish cannons?*
3. *How did Till signal the Spanish to fire their cannons?*

Clever Manka

This story comes from Czechoslovakia. Czechoslovakian tales are known for their humor and wit. The young woman in the story is known for her wit as well.

Petrovic was a rich farmer who lived in a small Czechoslovakian village. Not too many people liked him, and fewer still trusted him. He cheated and he lied. He made promises and often broke them.

Vaslov, a shepherd, was asked by Petrovic to tend his sheep during the winter. Petrovic agreed to give Vaslov a cow in return for his shepherding duties. Vaslov was trusting and, despite the warnings from friends, he went to work for Petrovic.

Spring came and Vaslov went to collect his cow, but Petrovic said that he had made no such deal. Vaslov felt sad and betrayed.

"We told you not to trust him," his friends told him. "You can't trust a man who has never kept a promise."

Vaslov felt worse and worse. Manka, his daughter, was the only one who didn't say, "I told you so." She told her father to take the matter up with the town's new burgomaster.

Vaslov took Manka's advice. When Petrovic heard that Vaslov had an appointment with the burgomaster, he then also made an appointment. The next day, both of the men appeared before the burgomaster.

The burgomaster was young and inexperienced, but he was fair. He listened to both cases without showing favoritism. He thought about it for a while and came back with a solution.

"You both have presented your cases well," the young burgomaster said. "So I have decided to give you a riddle to solve. He who gives the best answers will be awarded the cow."

Reluctantly, both men agreed.

"The riddle is this," the burgomaster said. "What is the swiftest thing in the world? What is the sweetest thing in the world? What is the richest thing in the world?"

The burgomaster told Petrovic and Vaslov to come back with answers the following morning. Each went away puzzled by the burgomaster's riddle.

Petrovic stormed into his house. He slammed the door and flopped down in his chair. "What nonsense this is," he growled. "What's the swiftest thing in the world? Indeed!"

His wife hurried into the room and sat in her chair, which was next to his. "What's wrong, my husband?" she asked.

"It's the new burgomaster. He's given Vaslov and me a riddle to solve. Whoever gives the best answers wins the case and gets the cow."

The farmer told his wife the riddle. She thought for a moment and then gave him her answers.

"Surely our gray mare is the swiftest thing in the world. She has been challenged many times but has never been beaten. As for what is the sweetest, have you tasted anything sweeter than our honey? Our chests of gold and silver must be the richest things in the world."

The farmer was thrilled. He was sure his wife had given him the winning answers.

"You are so right, my wife. The cow will remain ours."

Meanwhile, the shepherd went home, too. He was sad and upset. He was afraid that he wouldn't be able to solve the riddle in time.

"What's the matter, Father?" Manka

asked when she saw him.

"I am disappointed," Vaslov sighed. "I told the truth, and Petrovic lied. All the burgomaster gave us was a riddle to solve by morning. The best answers win the case. Petrovic is smart. I am sure he will have the right answers. Why even bother?"

"Oh, no!" Manka exclaimed. "We must try to solve it. What was the riddle?"

Vaslov gave her the riddle and went to sleep. The next morning, Manka gave her father her answers.

"These are good answers, Manka," he said, feeling more at ease. Then he set off to meet with the burgomaster.

When Vaslov reached the burgomaster's office, the farmer was already there looking as self-important as ever.

The burgomaster greeted both men. "Are you ready with your answers?" he asked.

The cheating farmer, sure that he had the right answers, went first.

"The swiftest thing in the world?" he began. "Well, that is my gray mare. She has never been beaten and passes everything on the road. The sweetest? The honey from my beehives is the sweetest I ever tasted. What is the richest? My chests of gold are the richest ever assembled."

With a smug expression, Petrovic sat down, rubbing his hands.

The burgomaster beckoned Vaslov for his answers. Vaslov bowed politely, which the farmer hadn't done, then gave his answers.

"Sir, the swiftest thing in the world is thought. Thought can run any distance as quick as a wink."

Petrovic chuckled slightly. He was now sure that he had won. "Thought, indeed!" he said to himself. Then he saw the smile on the burgomaster's face, and suddenly he wasn't so sure of himself.

Vaslov continued, "The sweetest thing in the world is sleep. When one is tired or sad, what could be sweeter than a good long nap? Finally, sir, the richest thing is the earth. Out of the earth come all the riches of the world."

The burgomaster stood up and clapped his hands. "Bravo!" he shouted. "Bravo! I award the cow to Vaslov, for he has given the best answers to my riddle."

Vaslov went to Petrovic's house and got the cow. Then he headed for home. He called to his daughter as he reached the gate. "Manka," he said, "your answers were the best. You are very clever to have thought of them so easily. I hope I am clever enough not to trust Petrovic ever again!"

1. *Why had Petrovic promised to give Vaslov a cow?*
2. *According to Vaslov, what is the sweetest thing in the world?*
3. *Who thought of the best answers?*

The Wooden Bowl

In this story from Italy, a young boy teaches his mother a valuable lesson, respect for the elderly. Versions of the story have been told for many years in Italian schools.

In a village in Italy, a young boy named Robertino lived with his mother, his father, and his grandfather. The boy's grandmother had died a little while ago. Robertino's mother and father had invited Grandfather Marco to live with them.

This made Robertino very happy because he loved being with Marco. The old man and the boy sang together. They ate together and played games. Marco told the boy wonderful stories, like the one about an eagle who took Marco to Mount Etna.

Julia, Robertino's mother, was always busy. Many times Robertino and Marco were in her way.

"Father," Julia would say, "why don't you make friends your own age? You would be out of the house some. Robertino would go out and play with other children."

The old man knew it was not easy for his

daughter to have this added person to take care of. Sometimes he was unsteady and needed help to get up and down. He needed food, of course, and he needed to have his clothes mended. Still, he enjoyed his time with the boy and he knew the boy liked his stories.

"I feel young when I'm around Robertino," Marco said.

Julia grew more and more impatient each day. One day Marco and Robertino were playing games in the living room before dinner. Julia called them three times. Then she came to get them.

"Will you two stop playing," she said. "Dinner is getting cold."

The two walked silently into the dining room and sat down at the table. The old grandfather was very unhappy that he was causing trouble again. As he nervously reached for a glass, he knocked his bowl onto the floor. The bowl broke into tiny pieces.

Marco became even more nervous and knocked over a water pitcher.

Julia began to shout. "If you cannot eat like a human being, then eat out there," she said. She pointed to the kitchen.

The old man excused himself and went to

Marco at dinner

the kitchen where he sat all alone.

Julia set a wooden bowl, wooden utensils, and a wooden cup before Marco. "Here," she said. "You can't break these!"

Robertino fought back angry tears. He couldn't understand why his mother was so upset with his grandfather.

"We all make mistakes," the boy said to himself.

Julia cleaned up the mess and swept the pieces of the broken bowl into the fireplace.

After dinner, Robertino tried to cheer up his grandfather. Marco was very sad.

"I am old and useless," he said. "I'm in the way, and I annoy my daughter." He walked slowly to his room and quietly shut the door.

A little while later, Julia found Robertino searching in the fireplace.

"What are you doing?" Julia asked.

"I'm picking out the pieces of the broken bowl," he answered.

"Why?" Julia asked.

"I'm going to put the pieces together," the boy said. "Then I'm going to get a block of wood and carve a wooden bowl like the broken bowl."

"Why do you want a wooden bowl?" asked his mother.

"So I can have a bowl for you when you get old and useless," Robertino said.

Julia was surprised. She knew her son did not mean to be disrespectful. She felt sorrow. Now she realized what it felt like to have one's own child say something cruel. She walked to her father's room and went in.

When Marco saw her, he asked, "Have I made you look so sad?"

"I am ashamed because of what I said to you," Julia said. "I should be much more understanding." A tear rolled down her cheek.

Marco smiled. "I am a foolish and frail old man," he said. "I must try to be much more careful."

The two of them walked down the stairs arm in arm. They wanted Robertino to know that everything was all right.

Marco called the boy, and they sat down together.

"It's time for another story, my boy," the old man said.

"I'd like to hear it, too," said Julia.

After that, the family all ate in the dining room. The wooden bowl became a special place to put flowers to remind them of beauty and love.

1. *Why had Marco come to live with Robertino's family?*
2. *Why did Julia make Marco eat in the kitchen?*
3. *Why was Robertino going to carve a wooden bowl?*

The Clockmaker of Strassburg

This tale is from the Rhine River valley in Germany. The town that was once Strassburg, Germany, is now Strasbourg, France.

The story has some basis in fact. There was a famous clockmaker in Strassburg who built a remarkable clock for the town. The rest of the story, however, is just that—a good story.

Guta's Choice

Long ago in the old town of Strassburg, Germany, there lived a clockmaker named Peter. He was so devoted to his beloved craft that he had time for little else. Peter sometimes forgot to eat. He seldom washed, and his clothes were tattered and torn. Guta, his only child, did try to take care of him, but it was difficult to do.

Peter's neighbors thought that he was quite strange. "He's not altogether sane," people would say when he and his daughter came to town. "In fact he's coo-coo, like his clocks!"

People did not care if Guta heard these

The clockmaker of Strassburg

unkind remarks. She often did, though, and they made her very sad.

Peter didn't seem to mind what other people thought of him. He knew that he was the best clockmaker in all of Germany, and that was all that mattered.

"Besides, Guta," he often said, "you and my work are all I need. I do not need to have people approve of me."

There was a man in the village who was very unpleasant. His name was Hermann. He was the fattest and the richest man in town. He had a bad temper, and he smelled just like spoiled sausage. The one thing he wanted was a beautiful wife, and Guta was his choice.

Hermann arrived at the clockmaker's cottage early one morning.

"I have been named the town magistrate," Hermann said boastfully. "I've decided to honor your daughter by asking for her hand in marriage. A man of my position and wealth needs a beautiful wife."

"What if Guta turns you down? What if I decide to turn you down?" Peter asked.

Hermann was shocked. "Turn me down!" he shouted. Then his mean little eyes grew narrow. "Then, as magistrate, I will declare you insane and send you off to prison," he hissed. "It would not be hard to do."

Guta listened in the kitchen as Hermann threatened her father. She was very fearful of this tyrannical man, but she wanted to save her father. She hurried into the room.

"I will marry you, sir, if it means saving my father from prison," she said sadly.

Peter was surprised at his daughter's agreement. He knew she had not thought about her answer carefully.

"Please, Hermann," he said, "give us two months to decide on our answer."

"All right," Hermann said. "I expect your answer to be the right one, however." He leered unpleasantly at Guta and then strutted out the door.

Peter had no intention at all of letting Hermann marry his daughter. In fact, Guta had already fallen in love with a fine young clockmaker from Bremen named Karl. Peter was fond of Karl and had thought of making him a partner. He knew Guta would never be happy with anyone but Karl.

The Clockmaker's Plan

Peter had a plan, and a month was all he needed to make his plan work. He had been working on a wonderful masterpiece. He would finish it in two weeks. This would leave more than a month before Hermann was to ask Guta to marry him again.

The clockmaker's masterpiece was a new timepiece for the cathedral steeple. It was an elegant clock, and it had many moving pieces that danced when the hour chimed.

"Breathtaking," sighed one young woman. "It is the most marvelous clock ever made."

"The clockmaker is quite talented, not insane at all," others remarked.

Within the week, word traveled across all of Germany about Peter's wonderful masterpiece. People came to see the clock, and businesses in the city of Strassburg flourished. Stores were crowded, and sales were brisk. Restaurants and hotels were full of people who had come to view the clock and also to hear it chime. Officials from The Clockmakers Guild proclaimed that the clock was the best ever made in Germany. They said that Peter was a true master.

Peter was in demand. Cities asked him to build clocks like the one in Strassburg.

Because of his newfound respect, Peter called for Hermann. He declared that Guta would not marry him. He said that Hermann should never come near Guta.

"You'll be sorry!" Hermann said angrily. "I'll make you pay for turning me down." He shook his fist and walked away in a huff.

Karl and Guta decided to marry at once. They were married in Strassburg Cathedral, as the magnificent clock struck six.

Hermann's Revenge

Hermann, as promised, sought revenge for what Peter had done. He met with the city officials of Strassburg.

"Every town now wants Peter to make one of his clocks," he began. "Where is the advantage in having every town in Germany with a clock such as ours? We will not be special if every town has the same clock. I don't need to remind you how much money has been made because of the clock."

A secret meeting was called. The city officials told Peter that for the good of the community he would have to cease making clocks. Peter refused because he was doing nothing wrong. Hermann persuaded the city officals to give Peter an unpleasant choice.

"Either stop working on clocks or we will blind you," Hermann announced.

Peter loved making clocks, and he would

never stop willingly. He decided that it would be better to lose his sight than to be so controlled.

"Take my eyes," he said, "but I have one last request before you do this. I must make a few minor changes in the clock."

The officials agreed. Peter made changes in the clock. Then Herman saw to it that Peter was made blind.

Soon the town became aware of the last-minute changes in their great clock. The changes caused the chimes to sound off-key. Other changes caused the clock to have the wrong time. Peter could not, of course, fix the clock since he could not see. Clockmakers were called in from all over Germany. None had the skill to fix the clock. Strassburg was to become known by the clock that never had the correct time.

Guta explained to the townspeople how Peter had lost his sight. Hermann and the others officials were chased out of town and never seen or heard from again.

Peter was content to have helped cause Hermann to leave Strassburg. He lived the rest of his life with his daughter and son-in-law. Karl had learned enough from Peter to become quite famous himself.

Peter wished many times that he had his eyesight. He felt he had lost it, though, for the love of his daughter and his work.

1. *In the beginning, what did the townspeople say about Peter?*
2. *Where was Peter's clock placed?*
3. *How did Peter's changes make the clock work?*

Pronunciation Guide

Every effort has been made to present native pronunciations of the unusual names in this book. Sometimes experts differed in their opinions, however, or no pronunciation could be found. Also, certain foreign-language sounds were felt to be unpronounceable by today's readers. In these cases, editorial license was exercised in selecting pronunciations.

Key

The letter or letters used to show pronunciation have the following sounds:

a	as in *map* and *glad*
ah	as in *pot* and *cart*
aw	as in *fall* and *lost*
ch	as in *chair* and *child*
e	as in *let* and *care*
ee	as in *feet* and *please*
ey	as in *play* and *face*
g	as in *gold* and *girl*
hy	as in *huge* and *humor*
i	as in *my* and *high*
ih	as in *sit* and *clear*

j	as in *jelly* and *gentle*
k	as in *skill* and *can*
ky	as in *cute*
l	as in *long* and *pull*
my	as in *mule*
ng	as in *sing* and *long*
ny	as in *canyon* and *onion*
o	as in *slow* and *go*
oo	as in *cool* and *move*
ow	as in *cow* and *round*
s	as in *soon* and *cent*
sh	as in *shoe* and *sugar*
th	as in *thin* and *myth*
u	as in *put* and *look*
uh	as in *run* and *up*
y	as in *you* and *yesterday*
z	as in *zoo* and *pairs*

Guide

Capital letters are used to represent stressed syllables. For example, the word *ugly* would be written here as "UHG lee."

burgomaster: BURG oh mas ter

Breman: BRAY men

Coulombiers: CO lum bee ERS

El Cid: el SID

Forez: FOR eyz

Geoffrey: JEF ree

Guta: Goo tuh

Guy: GEE

Haarlem: HAR lem

Jimena: hee MEY nuh

Kalevala: KAL uh val uh

Lorelei: LOR uh ly

Lusignan: LOO seen ahn

Mélusine: MEYL yoo seen

Muskens: MUS kenz

Pan Kotsky: PAN KOT skee

Petrovic: pet ROF ik

Phillipe: fee LEEP

Poititer: PWAH tee ehr

Poitou: pwa TOO

Reanault: ray NOH

René: re NAY

Reynard: ray NARD

Till Eulenspiegel: TIL OY len shpee guhl

Väinämöinen: VA ihn a muh ee nehn

Valencia: va LEN see uh

Vaslov: VAS lof